PICTURE DAY

MORGAN AND LINDA GRESKY

Illustrations by E. ASHER

Book Publishers Network
P. O. Box 2256, Bothell, WA 98041
425-483-3040 www.bookpublishersnetwork.com

10 9 8 7 6 5 4 3 2 1

ISBN   978-1-945271-76-2
LCCN   2017952303

Dedication

·⦿⧉⧈⧉·⧈⧉⧈·

To Parker Lee, Auron James, Emmylou Raye,

and all the sweet babies blessing our family.

Grow up to be silly!

And, a special, heartfelt thank you of love and

gratitude to our beautiful grandmother,

Jean Wasden.

Stanley is very excited. Today is picture day at school!

He wants to wear his favorite orange shirt.

Stanley holds it up proudly and sees that it is wrinkled. "I need to get these wrinkles out!"

·⚜·⚜·

"Maybe I can use a skateboard." But that doesn't work.

·•═══•·════·

"Maybe I can use a basketball."
But that doesn't work.

·◦⧉⧉⧉·⧉⧉◦·

"Maybe I can use a rolling pin." But that doesn't work.

"Maybe I can use a monster truck." But that doesn't work.

·⚬⟐⟐⟐·⟐⟐⟐⚬·

"Maybe I can use a kite."
But that doesn't work.

·ᴑᶓᶓᶁᶁ·ᶁᶁᶓᶓᴑ·

"Maybe I can use a pair of roller blades." But that doesn't work.

"Maybe I can use a trumpet."
But that doesn't work.

Stanley gives up.
Nothing is working.

Then Stanley's mom surprises him with a freshly ironed shirt. Stanley is thrilled.

Best picture day
EVER!

Building Creativity in your Child

·ᐅᖕᕝ᙭·᙭ᖕᕝᐊ·

Did you know that a study by the American Academy of Pediatrics says that play promotes creativity? Child educational psychologists suggest that engaging in creative activities with children helps them bond with parents, caregivers, and teachers. But, the benefits of creativity aren't limited to kids. Research indicates that creative activity contributes to successful aging by fostering a sense of competence, purpose, and growth.

So, how can you spark the creativity in your child now that will turn into a lifelong benefit later? It's easy. **Just be SILLY!**

Spontaneous — Look for any time opportunities to ask "what if" and "why" questions that spark a conversation. Build on your child's thoughts and ideas.

Imagination —There are no rules and keep it simple. Let the ordinary lead to the extraordinary. Allow enough time for unexpected twists and turns.

Laugh — It really is the best medicine. Support the creative process by participating in and appreciating that it really is fun.

Learn —The art of discovery can lead to a treasure trove of creativity. Meaning-making is a rich source for new insights.

Yes — Give permission to be free thinkers. Encourage creativity by cultivating an environment that embraces a playful spirit.

Now... Go Be Silly!

About the Authors

Morgan and Linda Gresky enjoying a road trip to Paris, Tx.

Living in Hillsboro, TX, this dynamic mother-daughter team loves fossil hunting, watching fireflies, photography, star-gazing, and exploring all the treasures Texas has to offer.